Consultant Gussie Hearsey on behalf of the Pre-school Playgroups Association

Aladdin Books
Macmillan Publishing Company
866 Third Avenue, New York, NY 10022
First published 1987 in Great Britain by Walker Books Ltd., London
First American edition 1988
First Aladdin Books edition 1989

Printed in Hong Kong by Sheck Wah Tong Printing Press Ltd.

A hardcover edition of *The Farmer* is available from
Macmillan Publishing Company.

10   9   8   7   6   5   4   3   2   1

Library of Congress Cataloging-in-Publication Data

Kightley, Rosalinda.
The farmer.
Summary: Simple text and illustrations describe a farm and the different jobs
performed by a farmer and his family.
1. Farmers—Juvenile literature. 2. Farm life—Juvenile literature.
[1. Farm life] I. Title.
S519.K45 1989   630   88–19431
ISBN 0–689–71222–7 (pbk.)

The Farmer

Rosalinda Kightley

Aladdin Books
MACMILLAN PUBLISHING COMPANY
NEW YORK

The farmer milks his cows at dawn,

Then he feeds the hens some corn.

The pigs get food

and fresh greens too,

The sheep are driven to pastures new

Next the farmer bales the hay,

Then plows his fields

for part of the day.

He picks ripe apples,

a bumper crop!

And digs up potatoes for the shop.

The Farm Shop

Then he clears the pond of weeds,

And gives the tractor the oil it needs.

At dusk he closes up the stable,

Then it's home for supper

at the kitchen table.